The Kaizen Journal

by

Kai Boyer

@the_kaizen_journal

Preface

The next 365 days is going to be a truly transformative process for you as an individual. My goal is to stimulate thought and open your mind to the possibilities of how you can put your best foot forward in aligning yourself in reaching your true potential. You will begin to notice you are becoming more self aware, considering new thoughts, feelings and ideas. It is a truly intimate and personal experience, each person will have a completely different transformational process.

Something magical happens when you regularly write down and connect with what you truly, and genuinely want in this life, it will start to manifest in different ways right before your eyes. With the right mindset, consistent habits and proper preparation your dreams will begin to become your reality.

The power to change your world begins with YOU.

@the_kaizen_journal

Opening Affirmation

Begin this journey of self improvement and personal development with an open mind and open heart. Be willing to consider and evaluate your short comings and fears with honesty and openness. Parts of this journey will be scary, uncomfortable and intimidating but know when you step outside your comfort zone that's where the growth and magic happens. No one is judging you or setting expectations for you, this is your own journey of self discovery it is what you choose to make of it.

Acknowledgment

To my family, friends and all the people that have supported me through this journey I am forever grateful.

Wishing you love, light and meaningful, powerful change along this journey.

Kai ♡

Day 1

Kaizen is the philosophy of small daily continuous improvements of ones self.

To begin this journey I want you to make a list of the 3 areas of your life you want to improve the most. It can be small gradual changes or it can be tackling a personal fear, whatever it may be I want each of your goals to be something that resonates with your heart.

Make your improvements small and gentle and you'll stick with them.

Day 2

There are many types of goals and dreams you will come to realize throughout this journey, Spiritual, emotional, physical and self discovery, which of these do you hope to improve the most through this journey and why? What does Kaizen mean to you?

Day 3

The Kaizen methodology is based on making little changes, monitoring the results and then readjusting. Having a strategic system for implementing small improvements yields great results in the long-term overall improvement.

What is the #1 thing you want to improve about yourself as a person? How can you go about a strategic system to interject these improvements just slightly into your everyday life?

Day 4

"The secret to getting ahead is getting started"
- Sally Berger

The toughest step in any journey is the first one, by beginning this book you have already taken the first huge step towards self improvement. The next step is implementing your goals into your every day life, what is your daily action plan for implementing this?

Day 5

Envisioning yourself in your end goal is so important. Once we create the vision it is much easier to work backwards and create a roadmap for your vision.

Where do you see yourself after 365 days of self improvement? What will it take to get there?

Day 6

There is often a lot of 'background noise' in our every day life that stops us from reaching our true potential by allowing it to distract us from our main goals and focus. What is the background noise in your life and how can you go about minimizing or eliminating it?

Day 7

What does 'forward progress' look like to you and how do you personally tangibility identify progress? (This is important to know what constitutes a win in your book)

Day 8

"Success is never a destination- it is a journey."
- Satenig St. Marie

Success is not a final destination that is ever reached, it is a constant journey of being ever evolving. How would you like to evolve as a person both personally and professionally?

Day 9

"Every day do something that will move you closer to a better tomorrow"- Douglas Firebaugh

It can start by doing just 1 push up, clearing out the house of junk food, deleting a social media app.

Pick just 1 thing today to set yourself up for success tomorrow.

Day 10

"Take one small step at a time don't try to do too much all at once or you'll be less likely to start. Be glad for your small accomplishments even if you're not perfect yet." -Eric Hudson

Biting off more than you can chew can be overwhelming and often leads to giving up on a goal. What does taking a small step or a continuous 1% improvement of one self look like to you?

Small incremental changes towards a goal
=   SUCCESS

Day 11

"The thing that is really hard, and really amazing is giving up on being perfect and beginning the work of becoming yourself." - Anna Quindlen

Have you come to accept yourself and your flaws (we all have them)? Are you comfortable in your skin with who you are as a person?

Day 12

"To stand still is to fall behind."- Gordon Forward

Continuous improvement of oneself is a never ending journey, what does continuous improvement look like to you?

Day 13

"Action is a great restorer and builder of confidence, inaction is not only the result but the cause of fear." - Norman Vincent Peale

What does taking action look like to you?

Day 14

"You have to expect things of yourself before you can do them." - Michael Jordan

Expectation drives the creative process, expecting more of yourself often leads you to try new things to get to your end goal.

What are some of the expectations you set for yourself?

Day 15

Tiny Wins build Confidence

What tiny win can you accomplish today that will make you feel good? It can be something small like just signing up for the gym not even attending yet.

Today I want you to focus on setting yourself up for future successes.

Day 16

"I cannot say whether things will get better if we change, what I can say is that they must change if they are to get better." - George Christoph Lightenberg

There is only one way to improve your future and it is to continuously grow, change and evolve, what are three things you would like to change in your life or about yourself in order to evolve into your ultimate self?

Day 17

"Overcome a fear and stagnation goes out the window"-Peter Shankman

Fear is often the #1 thing that holds people back from getting ahead, once fear is gone what holds you back from moving forward?

Day 18

"Success is 99% failure" - Soichiro Honda

The most successful people are usually those who have tried and failed more than any of us would have attempted. Why does failure scare you? What is the worst thing that can come of it?

Day 19

To win, you must begin
It all starts with the first step, what are two things
you have been wanting to do but putting off or
making excuses for not doing?

Day 20

"As long as the mind can envision the fact that you can do something you can do it." - Arnold Schwarzenegger

The mind is a very powerful tool, to be able to make something a reality you must first be able to picture it in your mind. What is something you have had in your mind that you would like to make a reality?

Day 21

"Change is inevitable, growth is intentional."
- Glenda Cloud

What are 3 of your reasons to embrace change?

Day 22

In Kaizen, problems are seen as opportunities to improve. What problems or areas do you run into that you would like to improve in your life, time management, productivity, interpersonal connections?

Day 23

Self Reflection

What 5 words would you use to describe yourself
currently?

Day 24

What does being disciplined mean to you? In what areas are you self disciplined? What areas would you like to be more self disciplined?

Day 25

Every actions begins with a thought. What thoughts would you like to turn into actions?

Day 26

Don't be afraid to start again, whether it's a new job, leaving a toxic situation or beginning a new chapter in your life. What would you like to start over?

Day 27

Today I want you to write down every aspect of the life you truly want, whether it's the type of partner you have, the car you drive, the job you have, the house you live in, every detail I want you to write it down in great detail.

Day 28

Reflecting back to yesterday's prompt

What is your core motivation for success? To have more freedom? To better provide for your family? Why do you have these specific goals in life? It is important to be clear what gets you motivated to get big results

Day 29

Why is personal development important to you?
What do you hope to achieve by the end of your
Kaizen journal?

Day 30

Short term goals- Where would you like to see yourself in 3 months? What about in 6 months?

You have just completed your first 30 days. WOW, You are POWERFUL!

Day 31

How do you feel about your physical appearance? What aspects about your physical health or wellness would you like to change?

Day 32

What is 1 new habit you would like to make a part of your daily routine? Whether it be flossing your teeth or making sure you exercise each day, how can you make sure it becomes part of your concrete plan. I recommend setting aside a specific time in your day to ensure this habit gets accomplished.

Day 33

What is one thing you have always wanted to learn more about? And how can you immerse yourself more into it. It can be cooking, learning how to sew, literally any skill you want to improve.

Day 34

Self improvement is an ongoing process. What are some small wins that you have had so far in the first month of your journey?

Day 35

Change can be scary, it means new patterns, new situations and new feelings.
Do you like change or find it difficult and uncomfortable? Why or why not?

Day 36

Are you holding onto people, emotions or things that no longer serve you or make you feel good? How can you work towards letting them go?

Day 37

Self Care

What is your favorite way to pamper yourself? Do you do it often enough? If you struggle with self care, what are the top reasons you neglect taking care of yourself? Time, energy, money?

Day 38

What is one affirmation that makes you feel the most empowered? Repeat it daily.

Day 39

"The most important relationship you have is with yourself. Everything happens in your life results from the way you treat yourself, through thoughts, words and actions." - Roxana Jones

What are three simple ways you can show yourself love every day?

Day 40

What do you feel like you need the most right now, and how can you meet that need?
For example, more alone time, better sleep at night, more exercise.

Day 41

Coping

How do you cope with stressful or overwhelming situations? How do you believe you could do a better job of handling them?

Day 42

What are 3 ways you plan to proactively feed your mind with positive, inspirational and prosperous thoughts and ideas?

Day 43

What boundaries do you need to set with others and yourself to prioritize your goals and self care?

Day 44

Write down your top 10 goals to complete by the end of this year. Also be sure to detail specific plans as to how you expect to execute your goals.

Day 45

Create an avatar.

Write down the type of person you wish you could be. What is their personality? Where do they work and live? How do they react to difficult situations? Think about ways you can bridge the gap between who you are now and the avatar you created.

Day 46

Author and motivation speaker, Jim Rohn, once said: Success is nothing more than a few simple disciplines, practiced every day.

Pick 2 new disciplines to develop, for example going to bed earlier, showing gratitude each day, meditating each day. They can be small and simple to start.

Day 47

Your best self is rooted in your personal wellness. Wellness is comprised of seven dimensions <u>spiritual, intellectual, occupational, emotional, physical, sexual and social.</u> While all of these are interrelated and impact each other, you can work to improve each area individually. Each one of these are connected to the core of who you are, what you believe and your purpose in this world. It is from here that your true impact will grow and your wellness will blossom.

List these dimensions 1-7 in order of importance to you and which ones you would like to improve the most.

Day 48

READ and your wisdom and inner peace will grow.

What are three new things you have learned or started doing as a result of reading? What was the last inspirational/motivational book you have read?

Day 49

Spiritual wellness and health = LOVE.

The more we love ourselves and others and the more beauty in our circumstances we perceive as well. The more we focus on our spiritual health and wellness, the more love we will feel alive and in control of our lives.

What can you do to improve your spiritual health and wellness?

Day 50

The biggest barrier to connecting with inner peace is stress and anxiety. We often think stress comes from external sources but when we realize that stress is how we perceive and react to it we can create a healthier relationship with it.

When our lives are stressed and we don't create opportunities to recharge and connect with ourselves in solitude, we go into survival mode.

What can you do to find more inner peace and have less stress and anxiety in your daily life?

Day 51

As leadership expert John C. Maxwell stated "You will never change your life until you change something you do daily. The secret to success is found in your daily routine."

Write out your daily routine, from how long you read the news, how much time you spend watching tv, note what areas do you believe could be cut out and be a more efficient use of your time.

Day 52

Notifications and distractions in today's world we are constantly bombarded by our phones and computers going off with every text, email, social media notification, amazon tracking and so much more. Each time our phones go off we tend to stop what we are doing to check to see what the latest update is and more times than not it is something that does not require our immediate attention.

What are 3 ways you can cut down on distracts in your daily routine? One of the ones I found most successful was turning off all notifications for everything that didn't need to urgently be handled IE instagram, facebook, etc

Day 53

Identify 3 new positive habits that you would like to form to get you on track for reaching your ultimate goal.

Day 54

You can't achieve success without knowing your destination. Having a vision of where you want to go makes it easier to create a road map and develop a plan for focused action.

Based on your vision, create long term goals and list. Ensure that they are meaningful goals that inspire you to think big and build your commitment to stay on course no matter what obstacles you face along the way.

Set tangible guidelines for you to review your goals. (Recommended review your short term goals at the beginning of each month. Year long goals, every quarter. Long term goals, the end of year.)

Day 55

Beliefs are what drives a person to be who they are and act in certain ways especially under pressure. What are your beliefs, do you always stay true to them?

Day 56

There are things in life we must do and things in life we want to do. There is a balance between doing things like going to work, doing chores and things like hanging out with friends or taking vacations that we like to do.

What would you like to do more of?

What would you like to do less of?

Day 57

Pacing yourself in everyday life so you do not burn out is so important.

How is the pace of your life? How do you believe you could create a better balance in your life?

Day 58

Choose wisely what you give your time, love and energy to. Where are you putting your energy? Is it paying off or do you feel that is it draining you?

What activities drain your energy the most?

What activities give you energy?

Day 59

Visualization Activity: Close your eyes and visualize what you want your life to look like in one year.

Where are you? What do you do for work? Are you in a relationship? Try to picture every detail. This can help us realize what our truest hopes are.

Day 60

Sleep, Rest & Recovery

So many of us don't get enough rest. We are bombarded by work and end up doing things like drinking more caffeine to get us through the day.

Do you sleep enough? Having a set bedtime and evening routine, calming your mind and body before bed has significant impacts on how rested you are and therefore more productive the next day.

Day 61

Creating a positive environment comes from being in an uncluttered space both mentally and physically, what are some things you can do to rid yourself of both types of clutter?

Day 62

Self love is so important, for others to love and accept you, you must love and accept yourself first. Many of us especially women tend to be hypercritical of ourselves, our appearances, our skills and it is a negative self talk circle to be in.

Are you kind to yourself? How could you be more accepting of yourself and do a better job of being self confident in your abilities?

Day 63

Perhaps the greatest standout quality of people with exceptional character is how they inspire others nearly effortlessly. Everything about these types of people make them stand out from the rest. (entrepreneur.com)

Who is one person in your life that truly exhibits exceptional characteristics? What qualities about them do you admire the most?

Day 64

Work ethic is one of the most important factors to a person's success in life. Do you have a strong work ethic? Why or why not?

Day 65

It is often said that religion is belief in someone else's experience, spiritually is having your own experience. How have your own experiences whether they are good or bad shaped your beliefs and outlook on life? Are you spiritual or are you religious?

Day 66

What quote inspires you the most? What does it mean to you? Write it down and put it somewhere that you will see it each day.

Day 67

Are there parts of your life that you find distracting or a waste of time/energy?

How can you improve upon them or cut them out of your life?

Day 68

Self reflection is huge in the growing process, seeing your own strengths and weaknesses as a human. Do you take the time to reflect on what is happening in your life? Hint: journaling is a great way to self reflect on your life and habits.

Day 69

Life begins at the end of your comfort zone.

When was the last time you did something outside your comfort zone.
How do you feel outside of your comfort zone?
Do you feel more alive? Do you feel scared?

Day 70

"Success without fulfillment **is** the ultimate failure."-Tony Robbins.

Do you find your life fulfilling? What could you do to feel more fulfilled by your successes?

Day 71

Procrastination is the opposite of progress. Are you putting any parts of your life on hold?

If so what is holding you back, fear, laziness, lack of motivation?

Day 72

Courage is Grace under Pressure.

Do you believe you work well under pressure? Do you believe you handle stressful situations well?

Day 73

"When you improve a little each day, eventually big things occur. When you improve conditioning a little each day, eventually you have a big improvement in conditioning. Not tomorrow, not the next day, but eventually a big gain is made. Don't look for the big, quick improvement. Seek the small improvement one day at a time. That's the only way it happens and when it happens, it lasts." - John Wooden

What makes the Kaizen Method so effective?

Day 74

Showing gratitude and being grateful for the little things in your life is so important, what are you most grateful for? How can you express more gratitude in your life? It can be something small like sending a text or card to someone that you appreciate.

Day 75

There are 8 billion people on this planet and no two are exactly alike, every single one is a unique and special individual. What makes you unique? How can you share more of your gifts with the world?

Day 76

Name 3 unique skills, talents or qualities you have that truly sets you apart, it can be simple like being able to connect or empathize with people.

Day 77

Exercise is a great way to improve your cortisol levels and improve mental clarity and focus. When was the last time you really pushed yourself in a physical activity? How did you feel after?

Day 78

What is one personality trait you are aware of that you need you need to improve upon?

For example: anger, patience, understanding, empathy

Day 79

Failing is not the worst thing in the world; quitting is.

Do you believe you give up easily on things?
What makes you feel like you cannot achieve it?

Day 80

"You must be who you really are, then, do what you need to do in order to have what you really want." - Magaret Young

Do you believe you portray who you really are or do you feel that you are expected to act/ speak a certain way?

Day 81

Interpersonal relationships, being able to communicate, share and talk with others is one of the main pillars of our social constructs. What would you like to improve in your interpersonal relationships? Whether it be being able to communicate your feelings or be more open with those you love

Day 82

"Your life is a mirror that doesn't lie, so look at your present self and ask yourself is this where I want to be?" - Bonnie Hall

If your answer is no, what can you do to put yourself in a more positive or beneficial situation starting today?

Day 83

What do you need to make more time for in your weekly routine?
Self care, exercise, spending time with family?

Be sure to concretely block out at least an hour on your schedule every week for this activity.

Day 84

"Each day you can choose your thoughts, actions and where you put your attention." - Day Mata

Where did you put your attention today?

Day 85

"Innovation comes from believing that everything has the potential to be improved."
 - Robert Dennard

What is one thing you want to innovate in your life?

Day 86

You communicate power through body image and how you present yourself. Standing tall, walking proudly and presenting yourself as confident are are powerful images.

What body language and signs do you give off?

Day 87

"Success is a staircase not a doorway."

What does this quote say to you about Kaizen and continuous improvement?

Day 88

Disconnecting especially in todays world is often a much needed break- when was the last time you disconnected from social media, your phone and technology?

Spend 1 day without social media and minimal technology and see how you feel, does your productivity increase are you more clear minded?

Day 89

Self Discovery

It is a never ending process, you continue to grow, change and evolve. We learn new things about ourselves usually in big moments whether they are good or bad. When was the last time you discovered something new about yourself?

Day 90

Reflection Time!

You are officially a quarter of the way there!!

What changes have you noticed about yourself so far, mentally physically or emotionally?

What areas do you believe you need more focus more on?

Day 91

Meditation is a great time to focus on your thoughts, inner feelings and emotions. When was the last time you meditated?

Spend 10 minutes today meditating and clearing your head of worries and anxiety.

Day 92

Breathing is essential to life, it relaxes and calms us especially when we focus on deep breathing, inhaling in through our belly and exhaling out through our mouths.

Take 5 minutes to focus on your breathing and calming your thoughts

Day 93

Self Control
The only person you can control is yourself.

How can you set the best example for the people around you in your behaviors and actions?

Day 94

"Enthusiasm gets you moving, passion helps you gain mastery and desire keeps you in the game. Before you know it your enthusiasm, your passion and your white hot desire will lead you to success." - Ivan Mismer

Enthusiasm and passion are two of the greatest factors to ones success, finding something in life that you are both passionate and enthusiastic about is crucial to success. What areas or things are you most enthusiastic about?

Day 95

"Tears will get you sympathy. Sweat will get you results."

This quote says a lot about your attitude towards handling difficult situations, how do you face adversity?

Day 96

What is something you want to bring into your life?

Hint: writing what you want in your life helps to concretely understand it and therefore manifest it faster.

Day 97

"You'll never have all the information you need to make a decision, if you did it would be a conclusion not a decision." - David Mahoney

What does this quote say to you about never being 100% sure of a decision until it is in hindsight?

Day 98

"Don't discard your fantasies as merely wishful thinking, honor them as messages from the deepest part of your being about what you can do and directions you can chose."
- Sanage Roman

What was one of your latest fantasies that led the direction that you chose?

Day 99

"Life is like an ever shifting kaleidoscope a slight change and all patterns alter."
- Sharon Salzburg

Perspective has a lot to do with how people view situations and how they react to them. What does this quote say to you about perspective and how viewing things differently could change your entire perspective?

Day 100

"Worry is a misuse of the imagination" - Dan Zadra

Worry and anxiety is time consuming and a waste of brain capacity that often stifles creativity and critical thinking and leads to poor decision making. What is one thing you often find yourself worrying about?

Day 101

"It takes the hammer of persistence to drive the nail of success"- John Mason

What does being persistent mean to you?

Day 102

"You may be on the right track but don't just sit there or you'll be run over."

This quote speaks to never being complacent or standing still. What does it look like to always be hungry?

Day 103

Productivity and time management often separates the good from the great. Are you good at organizing your time? What could you do to improve your time management skills?

Day 104

"Nothing worthwhile ever happens quickly and easily. You achieve only as you are determined to achieve and as you keep it until you have achieved." -Robert Lauer

The best things in life are often difficult to achieve, what does this quote say about commitment??

Day 105

"Whatever you are in life starts with what you think you are." - Jim Calhoun

Believing in yourself in yourself is half the battle, how do you think of yourself?

Day 106

"Dreams are maps. The ability to think about the future is what drives us all to attain."
- Irwin Redlener

What was a dream recently that stood out significantly to you?

Day 107

"When you change the way you see things, you change the things you see." - S. Wright

This quote talks about perspective and attitude, remember the saying your glass is either half full or half empty? How can you have a more positive and optimistic outlook on life?

Day 108

Self-improvement isn't a destination. You're never done. Even if you have some success, if you want to maintain it, you have to keep doing the things you were doing that got you that success in the first place.

What can you do to keep yourself from becoming complacent?

Day 109

Kaizen focuses on eliminating waste in your life or in processes to further productivity.

What do you consider to be a "waste" in your life that you would like to get rid of?

Day 110

Consciousness

You have to be aware of yourself, your tendencies, your strengths and shortcomings in order to improve.

What things are you conscious of that you would like to improve about yourself? For example: Following through with projects, staying on track with exercising and dieting.

Day 111

Whatever you hold in your mind on a consistent basis is exactly what you will experience in your life.

What do you often find yourself thinking about?

Day 112

When was the last time you did something for yourself that made you happy? Why did it stand out to you?

Day 113

Journaling every day can drastically help develop your mental clarity deepen self-awareness as well as increase your productivity and performance.
What are 3 things that you have noticed better clarity in your life since your journaling transformation?

Day 114

Self -Actualizing - *noun*

The realization or fulfillment of one's talents and potentialities, especially considered as a drive or need present in everyone.

What does self- actualizing mean to you?

Day 115

The place of change is in the brain.
Our reality is largely a perception of what we have going on in our brains, whether we view it positively or negatively.

What is one thing you would like to change in your brain? Whether it's negative or anxious thoughts or how you react to situations.

Day 116

"Life expands or shrinks based on ones courage"
- Anais Nin

Often times it takes much courage to seize an opportunity for something great to happen, do you believe you are courageous?

Day 117

"I cannot say whether things will get better if we change, what I can say is that they must change if they are to get better." - George Christoph Lightenberg

There is only one way to improve your future and it's to continuously grow, change and evolve, what are three things you would like to change in your life if you could instantaneously?

Day 118

Self Control

What area of your life would you like to have more self control in? It can be binge eating, not exercising enough, shopping too much.

Day 119

"Geniuses swim, crazy people drown. Most of us are sitting safely on the shore. Take a chance and get your feet wet." - Michael J. Gelb

What does this quote say about being willing to take a chance for success?

Day 120

Name 3 ways your life is wealthy, abundant and prosperous.

Day 121

If you could pick one thing in the world to change what would it be? Why?

Day 122

You're at your happiest when you . . .
(finish that sentence and true think about when
you are your happiest)

Day 123

What is one physical feat you have always wanted to accomplish? Whether it be 50 push ups or doing 2 consecutive pull ups. How can you start today working towards that goal?

Day 124

Experiences create unforgettable memories, what is one unforgettable experience that you have done or want to do?

Day 125

Being outside in nature is therapeutic to our mind, body and spirits. When was the last time you went out in nature?

How do you like to experience nature?

Day 126

"Striving for excellence motivates you, striving for perfection is demoralizing."- Harriet Braiker

No one is perfect, the best we can do is strive for excellence and being our best selves. Do you believe you strive for excellence or perfection?

Day 127

Self care is so important to making ourselves feel LOVED

Pick your favorite self care source whether it is a bubble bath, a massage or a girls day and love yourself.

Day 128

What would your highest self say to your current self? (Your highest self being your future, evolved, self.)

Day 129

What is one bad habit you need to rid yourself of? it can be biting your nails, consuming too much junk food, going to bed too late.

Make a solid and specific game plan as to how you can kick that habit.

Day 130

Create a bucket list - 5 things you would like to do
or accomplish in your lifetime.

Day 131

What is you biggest fear in life? What can you do to conquer it

Day 132

Are you happy with your current relationships? Do you believe you surround yourself with peers and mentors who cause you to elevate your mindset ?

Day 133

Passion is the start of everything great. When you are passionate about something you give it that much thought and attention. What are you most passionate about?

Day 134

"Foster an atmosphere of trust, always be open to new sources of information and expect answers to come from the most unexpected of places."
- Krishna Venkatraman

Do you believe you are open minded? When was the last time you unexpected learned something new?

Day 135

What does self love and self acceptance look like to you? What is one thing you would like to be able to love and accept more about yourself?

Day 136

"The future is not something we enter, it is something we create." -Leonard I. Sweet

Each of our future's is largely in our own hands, what do you hope to create in your future?

Day 137

Trial and Tribulations
Everyone goes through highs and lows in life, in the moment it can often seem like there is no clear path out.

When was the last time you had a low and what did you learn from it? Most importantly how did it make you grow?

Day 138

"The energy it takes to hang on to the past is holding you back form a new life."
- Mary Manin Morrisey

Anger, resentment, frustration are all negative emotions and feelings that hold you back. What would let go of today?

Day 139

"You make your own luck by being prepared for opportunities" - Tony Paradiso

Being prepared and being ready to welcome new opportunities with gratitude is half the battle, how can you be better prepared?

Day 140

Creativity is a great way of self expression beyond words.

What is one new creative hobby you would like to try? For example coloring, painting, or cooking are all great forms of self-expression

Day 141

What goals or aspirations have you let fall by the wayside?

How can you do a better job of actively putting them in your routine?

Day 142

Evaluating your 'True Self' and who you hope to become at the end of this journey.
Do your current goals align with your core values? Why or why not?

Day 143

"The world needs your dreams. It's never been a better time to take a stand for what matters to you most." - Marcia Weider

What is three things in the world you would like to change if you had the power to?

Day 144

"Winners do things losers don't want to do."

What is something you don't want to do but know you must do to succeed?

Day 145

"If you love what you do then the world will fall in love with you." -Chuck Williams

Do you love what you do? What would be your dream job that you would wake up excited for every single day?

Day 146

In order to consider others we must first be self aware of ourselves and how our thoughts and actions can affect others in our lives.

What does self-awareness mean to you? How can you become more self aware and conscious of how your thoughts, words and actions affect those around you?

Day 147

Being spontaneous can be fun and exciting, when was the last time you spontaneously did something fun?

Day 148

Inner peace is finding the quiet, content, inner happiness within ourselves.

What does inner peace look like to you? When was the last time you had inner peace?

Day 149

What are your biggest time wasters in your day?
What distractions are hindering your productivity?
How can you reduce them?
Hint: only allowing a set time for social media or
watching TV is hugely helpful in this area

Day 150

It takes very little extra to be extraordinary,
 what opportunities or ways can you push yourself
a little bit extra today to be extraordinary?

Day 151

What habits, memories, relationships = 'baggage'.
are you holding onto that are keeping you from
improving yourself?

How can you free yourself of these weights?

Day 152

Only one thing has to change for us to know happiness in our lives: where we focus our attention.

Where do you find yourself focusing your thoughts and attention? Are they towards growth and expansion or are they towards negativity and frustration?

Day 153

How can you brighten up your loved one's day today?
It can be something simple like sending a simple note of appreciation or preparing a homemade meal.

Day 154

"If you don't control your life, don't complain when others do" - Beth Mende Conny

Do you believe you are in control of your life, why or why not? What could you do to be in better control of your life?

Day 155

"Nobody will believe in you unless you believe in yourself." - Liberace

We are all our own greatest critic but it is important to also be your own biggest fan. What does believing in yourself look like to you?

Day 156

"Challenge is a dragon with a gift in its mouth. Tame the dragon and the gift is yours."
 - Noela Evans

This quote speaks about patience, when was a time that being patient paid off for you?

Day 157

A powerful person is a master networker. Good networking increases your visibility and gives you a valuable circle of people to give and receive support from.

How do you feel about your network? Are they bringing you up or holding you back?

Day 158

"The longer you wait to decide what you want to do, the more time you're wasting. It's up to you to want something so badly that your passion shows through in your actions." - Derek Jeter

What does inaction and spending too much time contemplating a decision look like to you? How can you force yourself to move forward?

Day 159

"Achievement seems to be connected with action. Successful men and women keep moving. They make mistakes but they don't quit."
 -Conrad Hilton

This quote speaks about always moving forward despite failures and mistakes, what does this mean to you? (Kaizen)

Day 160

What is your biggest insecurity? How can you work to come to terms with it and overcome it? can you meet your insecurities, mistakes, and flaws with grace, acceptance, and love?

Day 161

Repetitive complaining will attract things for you to complain about.

Repeat gratitude will attract things for you to be thankful about. What things in your life are you most grateful for?

Day 162

What are your three biggest pet peeves? Why do these triggers or actions bother you so much?

Day 163

What can you start today to move you closer to your goals? (even just 1% improvement)

Day 164

What makes you feel most alive? And when was the last time you felt that way?

Day 165

Keeping all parts your brain stimulated is so important, what are some different ways you like to keep your brain engaged? Crossword puzzles, jeopardy, memorization are all great ways to keep your brain engaged.

Day 166

If you want your body to perform at its peak you must be vigilant about only giving it the highest quality ingredients.

 Do you believe you consume healthy food, what things could you do to have a better and healthier diet?

Day 167

One of the most difficult parts of self care is dedication and taking the time away from your busy schedule to focus on yourself. However giving yourself 5 even 10 minutes to really focus on how you are feeling is good for your soul and spirituality.

When you start to feel overwhelmed or burned out what can you do to reflect inwardly?

Day 168

"Conflict is growth trying to happen."
- Mary Bellofatto

Internal conflict is often times between wanting to try something new and also being afraid what can happen, what was the last time you had conflict? Did it lead to growth?

Day 169

"Making the best of ourselves is the reason we were born, but it requires patience and perseverance." - Sarah Ban Breathnach

What does being patient and preserving look like to you?

Day 170

If your success was inevitable (which it is by the way) what would you do?

Day 171

Who is the person that is your biggest inspiration?

Why do you respect them so much? What are their core values?

Day 172

There are many forms of self care that help our mental well being besides meditating. Journaling, walks, bubble baths. What do you do for your mental well-being?

Day 173

What activities sets your soul on fire? (If you aren't sure, then think back to your childhood. What did you love to do as a kid?)

What makes you so passionate at it?

Day 174

The truth is that there is nothing in being superior to somebody else. The only real nobility is in being superior to your former self.   -Whitney Young

What do you look like in your ultimate 'superior' self?

Day 175

"People who are constantly killing time are really killing their own chances in life."
- Arthur Brisbane

This quote speaks about wasting time and opportunities, do you believe you waste time? If so doing what?

Day 176

"Suffering over things that have happened in the past is nothing more than an argument with the past." - Byron Katie

What is the one thing you look back on and find yourself suffering the most about? What would it take for you to let go of that pain and angst?

Day 177

Personal change is difficult but doable as long as you accept that its hard to satisfy your toughest critic - yourself.

What change would you like to see most about yourself and how would you measure successful change?

Day 178

Communicating is a sense of personal power that comes from the belief that you can reach your goals in your own way. Powerful people empower others and encourage others to express themselves openly.

How can you better empower others around you to living up to their true potential?

Day 179

"When we were children, we used to think that when we were grown-up we would no longer be vulnerable. But to grow up is to accept vulnerability." - Madeleine L'Engle

What does being vulnerable look like to you?

Day 180

"There are two things over which you have complete dominion, authority and control - your mind and your mouth."- Molefi Kete Asante

Which one of these two do you struggling more with?

Day 181

The Ladder of Success

1. Plan Purposely

2. Prepare Prayerfully

3. Proceed Positively

4. Pursue Persistently

Which one of these steps on the ladder is the most challenging to you?

Day 182

Benchmark - You are officially half way there!

Visualize yourself at the end of your 365 day Kaizen Method Self Improvement Journey.

What does your life look like? What have you let go of or released? What positive things have you brought into your life?

Day 183

Physical and mental health often go hand and hand. When we do not feel good about ourselves physically we often spend a lot of time thinking negative thoughts about ourselves and do not present with confidence. What could you do to make yourself feel better about your physical appearance?

Day 184

"Baby steps count. But you're always got to be moving forward." - Chris Gardner

What does this quote say about the Kaizen method?

Day 185

Managing your Stress and Anxiety.

Identify one way you best manage your stress or anxiety. Is it going for a run? Taking a bath? Knowing how you best cope with your emotions can help you better navigate them in the future.

Day 186

Close your eyes and think visualize yourself in a beautiful safe place such as the ocean or sitting in a field of flowers. Take a moment and transport yourself to this place.

What is something you smell? What is something you see? What do you hear?

Day 187

Inspiration is all around us and all within us.

What was the last thing you saw or did that made you feel inspired?

Day 188

Reflection Time

Looking back five years are you where you thought you would be? Have you accomplished what you set out to do? What about you is different how have you changed or evolved?

Day 189

"Either you decide to stay in the shallow end of the pool or you go out in the ocean."
- Christopher Reeve

You don't achieve great things in life by not taking risks, what is something you would like to do that scares you?

Day 190

Productivity planning is choosing to live life with intention every day. To be mindful and protective of our time and energy on the most micro level to slowly but surely win our macro goals of life.

How could you live with more intention?

Day 191

How can you improve your happiness level? By connecting with others, doing things you are passionate about, choosing to be positive and making the best of every situation.

Day 192

Gratitude Journaling

It can be done anytime during the day, but I'd recommend doing it in the morning before beginning your workday. Why? Because genuine gratitude reverberates into the rest of your entire day, setting off a domino effect of optimism with which you can approach your work, your clients, your family, and everyone else you cross paths with.

Journal 3 things you are grateful for in your life this morning

Day 193

What was the best thing to happen to you today?
Reflect on it.

Day 194

Meditation is a great first step toward self-improvement, self-awareness, and any kind of growth. Spend 10 minutes today meditating and focusing on being fully quiet inside.

Day 195

Let's study our day: what we have managed to do, how we were distracted, how we could improve on tomorrow?

Day 196

If I were to improve upon myself one thing physically what would it be? What could you do daily to get you closer to your goal?

Day 197

What currently brings you the most joy and happiness? How can you work towards doing more of it?

Day 198

Keep in mind you cannot see what you do not look for and you cannot look for what you don't believe in. You must always be looking for new opportunity, if you wander through life blind, you will never see the opportunity.

What does keeping your eyes open mean to you?

Day 199

Defining your limits
Set specific intake limits for yourself to get you ton track with reaching your goals. These can be both physical and mental

For example I will consume no more than 1 hour of TV 2x a week, I will have no more than 1 caffeinated beverage per day.

(Hint defining your limits and staying on track with them is hugely powerful)

Day 200

Relationships are all about balance. Identify positive traits that you bring to a relationship. This can help you focus on all that you have to offer.

Day 201

What would you attempt in this life if there was no chance of failure and why?
Is fear, resources or time what's holding you back?

Day 202

Habits often define our success, speaking or writing down a goal but not having the habits or will power to put in the effort to get us there will lead to failure.

Identify three new habits that will align and put you on track for reaching your end goal

For example, going to the gym at least 3x per week, meditating daily, cooking dinner at home more often.

Day 203

In Kaizen the smallest disciplines and littlest changes in ones life that gradually add up to the greatest triumphs. What is one small change you can start TODAY that will get you that much closer to your end goal?

Day 204

What is one behavior holding your back from living your best life? (it can even be scrolling too much on social media, drinking too much on the weekends etc.)

Day 205

Do you feel happy with your health and wellness routine? Why or why not and how can you do a better job of sticking to it?

Day 206

Expressing yourself creatively reduces the risk of disease and illness while simultaneously strengthening your health and wellness.
When was the last time you did something creative?

Day 208

We all have heard the benefits of sunlight and how being outside helps to boost our immune systems through Vitamin D. When was the last time you explored the world around you? Whether it be a hike or a walk on the beach?

Day 208

"There are no secrets to success, don't waste time looking for them. Success is the result of perfection, hard work, learning from failure, loyalty to those for whom you work and persistence." - General Colin Powell

While there is no are no secrets to success what is your winning formula to success?

Day 209

Assertiveness
The behavior that is active, direct and honest. It communicates an impression of self-respect and respect for others.

By being assertive we view our wants, needs and rights as equal with others. When was the last time you were assertive and how did it make you feel?

Day 210

Perseverance. Purpose. Pragmatism. These are qualities that translate ambition into achievement. - Nitin Nohria

What 3 words would you choose to describe the path between ambition and achievement?

Day 211

List your 10 favorite (and best) qualities about yourself:

Day 212

Destiny is not a matter of chance its a matter of choice. - William Jennings Bryan

Things don't happen by accident, what is one thing in your life that you have made a choice about and has lead you to your destiny whether it be good or bad?

Day 213

"Change your thoughts and you change the world" - Harold Mcalindon

Your thoughts control the world you participate in, they affect how you process and react to situations. What does changing your thoughts or outlook look like to you?

Day 214

Only you can be yourself. No one else is qualified for the job.

What does this quote mean to you about being yourself and being comfortable in your own skin?

Day 215

To evolve as an individual, feeding your mind with new ideas and information is essential. Every day, dedicate at least 15 to 30 minutes to reading material that enlightens and enhances your knowledge. Consume content that is actionable and directly relates to your goals and aspirations.

Set a goal of reading at least 1 book that expands your horizons every month

Day 216

Self care is important even small things like taking a bubble bath or putting on a face mask can make you feel so reinvigorated.

What is one thing you can do today to give to yourself and make you feel refreshed and reinvigorated?

Day 217

What is one bad habit you would like to change by this time next year? How can you begin working towards it today?

Day 218

Write down ten positive affirmations that you can recite when you're overwhelmed by your insecurities and fears.

Day 219

What's one thing you've done (no matter how small) that you're proud of yourself for?
Explain in detail

Day 220

Mindset Change

How do you believe you could change your life by changing your mindset? How could you go about viewing situations in a more optimistic and positive way?

Day 221

If you could change anything in your life in an instant, what would it be and why?

Day 222

The human experience is about connecting with other people. Connection is what provides value and meaning to our lives.

When was the last time you deeply connected with someone?

Day 223

"Tomorrow's success is yesterday's dream and today's perseverance." -Celia Jordaan

What does this quote say about getting started towards your dreams and not procrastinating?

Day 224

Lao Tzu, the ancient Chinese philosopher, once said, "He who knows others is wise; he who knows himself is enlightened."

Self-knowledge is about understanding your real (and true) needs, desires, goals, weaknesses, and everything else that makes you tick. It requires a deep understanding of your past and current self. Do you believe you have a good understanding of yourself, your needs, wants and desires?

Day 225

"One change makes way for the next, giving us the opportunity to grow."- Vivian Buchan

You never know where a single opportunity or change may take you, what is one change that would better prepare you for being able to capitalize on an opportunity that came your way?

Day 227

"If your spirit is very strong and you are in control of your thoughts, you are stronger than any fear."
- Susan Ryan Jordan

Do you believe you control your thoughts and fears or do they control you?

Day 228

On a daily basis what stresses you out the most?
Why do you feel this way?

What are some things you can do to alleviate the
stress?

Day 229

"Fail to take time now for your health and you will have to take time for illness later on."
- Donald Wetmore

Taking care of your health and physical body is so important, what have you done lately for your physical health and wellness?

Day 230

"Without a goal to work towards, we will not get there." - Natasha Josefowitz

Have you reviewed your goals lately, what are your daily goals? How well are you doing with implementing small steps daily getting you closer to reaching your goals?

Day 231

"Long-term commitment to new learning and new philosophy is required of any management that seeks transformation. The timid and the fainthearted, and the people that expect quick results, are doomed to disappointment."
- W. Edwards Deming

This quote speaks about the commitment to change, do you believe you are committed in the long term to the goals or do you expect them to happen over night?

Day 232

How can you add more adventure into your life? What is the one thing you want to change in your life to have more adventure? Where would you begin?

Day 233

What is one skill you wish you were better at?
How can you tangibly improve that skill?

Day 234

 What is one thing you can do today to improve your confidence in yourself?
This can be something small but it needs to be a concrete step in the right direction.

Day 235

If you could have anything in the world you would choose _____, because _____.
(It can be a super power, infinite life, whatever you choose.)

Day 236

PDCA Method

Plan and Recognize an opportunity for a change in your life (it can be something small like saying your positive affirmation every morning when you wake up)

- Do it. Test the change.

- Check. Review the test, analyze the results, and identify what you learned, how you felt as a result of the change.

- Act. Take action based on what you learned in the study step: If the change did not work, go through the cycle again with a different action plan. If you were successful, incorporate what you learned from the test into bigger changes.

Day 237

"Complacency stalks success as shadows stalk the sunlights."

What does this quote say about not becoming complacent?

Day 238

"People like nails lost their effectiveness when they lose their direction and start to bend."
- Walter Savage Landor

What does being 'effective' look like to you?

Day 239

What are some of the places on your bucket list to travel to? Make a list of them and why.

Day 241

Mindfulness, breathing meditation.
Most of us don't realize that when we are stressed out, we have a strong tendency to hold our breath and have shallow breathing.

By directing our attention to our breath, we not only take in more air, which relaxes our minds, but we bring our focus to living in the here and now. Focus on how your lungs expand with each in-breath, and contract with each out-breath. Let your breathing become relaxed and natural.

Day 242

At the base of Maslow's Hierarchy are those physiological needs: In short, you've got to make sure you're taking care of your physical health before you can approach spiritual wellness. Make self-care part of your practice: exercise, drink water, and eat right.

What have you done lately to take care of your physical health, spiritual wellness or self care?

Day 243

Volunteerism, mentoring, and giving back your communities can powerfully nourish you. Revisit those self-reflection questions to consider the values that drive you and how you exhibit them in your actions.

The most important aspect of spiritual well-being is believing in the aspect of giving rather than expecting.

Giving to others selflessly will give rise to a new positive outlook of life and you will feel more optimistic towards it. What can you do to give back to your community?

Day 244

Self Expression is a great way to showcase your unique thoughts feelings and emotions, what is your favorite method of self expression and how does it make you feel?

Day 245

What thought patterns have you noticed lately, and are they healthy or toxic?

Name 3 ways you can rid your life of bad habits, negative thoughts or needless activities?

Day 246

A healthy lifestyle is **essential for** longevity. Write down your physical activity goals for the week, IE 3 days of strength training, 2 days of cardio. Make your Goal list somewhere accessible that you will walk by each day, be sure you give yourself a check each time you complete an activity.

Day 247

Which core values do you live by and how do you
demonstrate them in your thoughts and actions?

Day 248

"Change is the process in which the future invades our lives." - Alvin Toffler

Change often leads us to a new destination and often times there is much pain and discomfort that comes with the process. When was the last time a shift pushed you to a different future than you expected?

Day 249

"When you cease to make a contribution, you begin to die." -Eleanor Roosevelt

Do you feel you are consuming or contributing to the world around you and why?

Day 250

As you begin your journey of self-awareness, you will find get more comfortable being your true self, transparent, and even vulnerable. You will create harmony between your current self and unconscious or true self. Becoming self-aware is the basic foundation for creating the life you want. Your happiness depends on it.

How can you become more self aware of your true self?

Day 251

"Happiness cannot be traveled to, owned, worn or consumed.Happiness is the spiritual experience of living every minute with love, grace and gratitude. "- Denise Waitley.

Happiness is not a final destination, it is a constant state of being each and every day. What does happiness look like to you?

Day 252

'Spiritual wellness is being connected to something greater than yourself and having a set of values, principles, morals and beliefs that provide a sense of purpose and meaning to life, then using those principles to guide your actions.'

What does this quote mean to you?

Day 253

"Power comes from living in the present moment where you can take action and create the future."
- Sanaya Roman

What does living in the present moment look like to you?

Day 254

Do you learn from your mistakes or just merely recover? Do you often find yourself making the same mistakes twice?

Day 255

Are you actively engaged in learning how to be a better person, friend, parent or spouse? Do you believe you actively support the success of the people in your circle?

Day 256

How do you make an effort to understand those from other backgrounds? Are you kind to those who are different from you?

Day 257

Yoga pairs elements of meditation and breathing with a full-body workout, a holistic approach hat increases flexibility, improves overall health, promotes better sleep and more, all while reducing stress and anxiety.

When wast the last time you did yoga? How did you feel after?

Day 258

What do you want to expand your knowledge in? What can you do to further your education on this subject? A book? A webinar? A seminar?

Expanding your mind is one of the greatest things we can do for our self development.

Day 259

Are you in control of your own emotions? Do you let others impact your emotional well being? Being aware of your triggers from others gives us power and the control to choose how we respond.

Day 260

"Luck is when preparation meets opportunity"

The complete formula to getting lucky

Preparation (personal growth) + Attitude (belief/ mindset) + Opportunity (a good thing coming your way) + Action (doing something about it) = LUCK

Which of these four areas do you believe you could work on the most to increase your LUCK?

Day 261

"Your thoughts are governed by the universal law of energy in what you focus in becomes your reality"- Debbie Bermont

Where you put your focus, thoughts and actions towards all gives off energy, the energy you give off is what you will receive back. Do you believe you give off good or bad energy? What makes you believe this?

Day 262

Mindfulness Daily

Practicing mindfulness is like regularly putting small amounts of change in a jar. They will all add up over time. And this will add up to greater peace and happiness.

What can you do on a daily basis to be more mindful? What does being mindful mean to you? Set it as a definite part of your routine

Day 263

If the sky was the limit who would you be? Go into detail and describe the best version of yourself.

Day 264

Do you let past dictate your future decisions? Is there something you struggle with? Either internally, emotionally or self consciously?

Day 265

Trust the Vibes you Get
Everything in this Universe gives off energy and vibrations, often times we try to use logic to overlook these feelings. When was a time you trusted your gut instead of your brain?

Day 266

What makes you feel bad or guilty? Is it when you eat bad or when you watch too much TV?
(It's important to identify these triggers).

Day 267

"Begin with determination to succeed and half the work is already done." - J.N. Fadenburg

Having determination and following goals through is one of the biggest factors in success. What are you most determined to do?

Day 268

What do you like to do to recharge your energy spiritually? Do you enjoy being alone or in a community for these experiences?

Day 269

How do you navigate challenges in life? What helps you to sustain in difficult times?

Day 270

Game Changing

We all have bad habits and behaviors we need to change to help get us in the direction of our ultimate desires. Eliminating bad habits from our lives helps us free up time and mental space for a new positive and more productive habit in its place.

What 2 habits do you need to get out of your life and what would you like to replace them with?

Day 271

Doing things that are ordinary is easy. Doing things that are extraordinary is what will separate you from the rest of the crowd.

What does being extraordinary and going above and beyond mean to you?

Day 272

"Your purpose in life is to find your purpose and give your whole heart and soul to it."
-Buddha

Have you found your purpose in life? Not all of us know quite yet so this may change with time as you find what truly sets your soul on fire.

Day 273

"Give yourself permission to dream big and risk big." - Darren Hardy

Greatness often takes sacrifice, some of the greatest people in history had to risk it all to be able to be successful. What big dreams do you have and are you willing to risk it all to achieve them?

Day 274

"Some want it to happen, some wish it would happen, others make it happen." - Michael Jordan

You cannot simply wish for success, you must be out there and willing to make it happen. What can you do in your power to guarantee your own success?

You are 3/4 of the way there! Be sure to review your goals and see that you are on track to reach them over the remainder of your journey.

Day 275

Decide right now to never settle for LESS again. Begin living the life you were MEANT to live.

Imagine yourself at your end goal, what path did you take to get there?

Day 276

Your time here is sacred.

You have been given this precious gift... of life.
Decide now the IMPACT you want to make today.

Write down 5 things that you could do today to
make your time more impactful.

Day 277

Exceptional Traits

To rise out of the ranks and out of the ordinary you must do things that set you apart from the other 99% of people on this planet, what are those traits?

Day 278

Many of us struggle to talk about how we are actually feeling and use coping methods to either hide it or deny that it is a real feeling.

Do you feel that you are a good communicator? What do you think you could do to improve your communication skills?

Day 279

When you have clarity, flow, momentum, flow and consistent habits, you can accomplish A LOT quickly. When you lack clarity, you get mired in excessive consumption and easily lost by distractions. How could you find more focus and clarity in your life?

Day 280

You must always be willing to truly consider evidence that contradicts your beliefs and admit the possibility that you may be wrong. Intelligence isn't knowing everything it's the ability to challenge everything you know.

When was the last time something or an experience changed your views or outlook?

Day 281

Today's life is hectic and full of stress hence being blissful is almost impossible with so many things going around you. The only way to calm your mind is by doing meditation which will relax your mind.

Pick a guided meditation track that best suits how you are feeling today.

Day 282

Show interest in others and appreciate the benefits of developing new, stimulating relationships. Recognize each person as someone you can learn from.

Find 2 people you find interesting or fascinating and have coffee/lunch with them and learn what makes them who they are. Human experience is often about learning and picking up things from people.

Day 283

Always acknowledge that your success in life has come with the help and support of many who believed in your ability and willingness to learn. Appreciate those who helped you get to where you are. (entrepreneur.com)

What is 3 ways you can show appreciation for the people that have supported and helped you along your journey?

Day 284

"Often it is the pain we experience that leads us not only to a different life but a richer, more rewarding one." - Dennis Wholey

What was the last painful experience that ended up leading to a better outcome for you?

Day 285

What gives you life meaning and purpose?
Family, friends, work? What brings you the most
inner peace and comfort?

Day 286

The benefits of meditation for your overall wellness including stress reduction, improved emotional health, boosted self-awareness and more.

Take 5 minutes out of your day today whether it be in the morning, on your lunch break or before bed to meditate and quiet all your inner busy thoughts.

Day 287

To be authentic you must operate without pretenses. Be confident and honest. Do not compare yourself to others and do not put any effort into being someone you are not.

Do you believe you portray your authentic self on daily basis or do you believe you're expected to act or present yourself in a certain way?

Day 288

Value your own time and the time of others. Be prepared, organized and efficient. In disciplining yourself to be organized and on time you will experience less stress. When you are on top of things life is more enjoyable. (entrepreneur.com)

What are 3 ways that you can be more efficient and effective in your work day?

Day 289

What are 3 things you'd like to change about yourself in the remaining 2 months of this journey? What 3 things have you changed so far?

Day 290

What has been on your mind lately (just starting writing and see what pops up)

Day 291

Live in optimism. Work on being self-competent. When you live through optimism you become an infectious person to be around. Strive to make other people feel good or better while in your presence. (entrepreneur.com)

What could you do to be more optimistic and how can you become more positively infectious to the people around you?

Day 292

Visualization

Take a minute and see yourself as your ultimate self. Who are you? What are you known for? How do you see yourself?

Day 293

Time Management

Making the most of your time each day. Many of us get lost in our phones and have no idea how many minutes and hours of our day we spend completely consumed in our phones, checking notifications, scrolling through social media, wasting countless hours and days of our lives with mindlessness.

Today I want you to set time limits in your phone for overall usage, time spent in each app. Your goal is to try to get this number down each week little by little and see what more productive things you can fill those minutes and hours with.

Day 294

What is 1 unwanted behavior you have been wanting to get out of your life? Whether it be kicking smoking or getting rid of a bad sugar habit.

How can you start today and ensure that you will stick to it. What will be your reward for succeeding or punishment for failing to uphold your behavior change.

Day 295

Do you believe in divine intervention? Meaning if something is not meant for you the universe will clear it away from you beyond your control. Has this ever happened to you?

Day 296

Physical Exercise Mindfulness

In order to perform an exercise to get the desired benefit, you need to use a proper technique. In order to use the proper technique, you need to pay close attention to how you are doing the exercise. In other words, you need to be fully present in the moment.

Another aspect of training that helps you live in the moment is tuning into what is happening in your body. First, during exercising, you need to pay close attention to how your body feels. Are you exercising hard enough, or not enough?

Day 297

What does sacrificing for greatness mean to you? What would you be willing to sacrifice to be great?

Day 298

Fear is the greatest reason most people do not live up to their full potential. What fear keeps you back most in life? Is it the fear of failure? Is it fear of judgement?

Day 299

One of the biggest keys of being able to see your future more clearly is to reverse engineer it. So let's think about that, if you were to write your obituary what would you want to be remembered as. Who were you a person, as a parent, as a friend? What were the things that stood out most in your life?

Day 300

'Without rain nothing grows. Learn to embrace the storms of your life.'

What was the biggest challenge you overcame in your life and how did you get through it?

Day 301

Do you believe you are highly productive both professionally and personally? If not what things do you think you could do to increase your productivity and effectiveness?

Day 302

"You may be disappointed if you try but you are doomed if you don't try." - Beverly Sill

What does this quote say to you about you about being afraid of failure?

Day 303

Spiritual Recreation

It's important to find time for whatever you find the most joy in! Whether hiking, cycling, connecting with new people, or dancing, intentionally make time every week. to do something that excites you at your core. Your spirit soars most in those moments, so be sure to find your 'spiritual recreation'.

What are three things you enjoy doing as a form of spiritual recreation?

Day 304

The practice of Mindfulness is about being fully aware of each moment in your life. Each thought, feeling, sensation and experience are accepted for what it is. There's no battle going on in your head and heart.

Mindfulness is often associated with meditation and being in the present moment.

What can you do be more mindful and fully immersed in each moment in your life?

Day 305

Openness increases your likelihood of developing relationships that are reciprocal, enduring and forward moving. How could you have more of an open heart and mind?

Day 306

"Always keep moving forward what you enjoy that is what gives your life meaning."
- Tom Welch

What gives your life the most meaning? Your work, family, friends, accomplishments?

Day 307

Ask yourself: 'Why am I not more successful than I am right now?'

What's been holding me back? What is one way to transform your adversity into success?

Day 308

Are you fueling your body correctly? What do you consume that makes you feel better? What makes you feel worse? What effort can you make today to fuel your body with good nutrients?

Day 309

Get outside more. We are inherently connected to the earth and all that encompasses nature. When we spend time outside and are surrounded by nature, our body relaxes, our breathing deepens and our minds calm. This helps us get in touch with our inner nature and authentic self.

When was the last time you were out in nature? How did it make you feel?

Day 310

"Have bold visions and audacious goals backed with relentless drive and courageous, consistent and obsessive action." -Darren Hardy

What does this quote mean to you about being a go -getter and putting action to your visions?

Day 311

Individuals who accomplish exceptional things never stop learning or growing. There's no 'I made it' moment. Exceptional people are life long learners, they are voracious readers, surround themselves with people who cause them to level up, and remain eternal students. No one is ever done growing, and there is no such thing as good enough when it comes to personal improvement.

What does it meant to be a life long learner and how can you expand your horizons of development more?

Day 312

Dealing with difficult people is frustrating and exhausting for most. Exceptional people are able to control their interactions with toxic people. When they confront a toxic person, they approach the situation rationally and often remove themselves from consistent interactions with them.

How do you handle toxic situations or relationships in your life? How do you believe you could handle them better?

Day 313

"Our minds becomes magnetized with dominating thoughts we hold in our minds and those magnets attract us to forces, the people, the circumstances of life which harmonize with the nature of our dominating thoughts." -Napoleon Hill

What we think about we become, everything we put into the universe comes back to us in some form. What does this quote mean to you about the importance of positive and productive thinking?

Day 314

When something isn't right for you, your soul rejects it and tries to warn you in many different ways. Always pay attention to what vibration things or people give you. These are all messages we should listen to, your body can pick up vibrations that your conscious mind cannot even perceive.

Do you believe you do a good job of listening to your intuition and trusting when something is not meant for you? When was a time you had a gut feeling about something but went against it anyway?

Day 315

What keeps you up at night? Is there a pressing problem you need to work out? Meditation or journaling before bed is a great way to compartmentalize and come to terms with your stressors, putting them on the shelf until the next day.

List 3 steps you can take towards solving this issue today.

Day 316

Self Reflection can help build self confidence. How do you describe yourself? What physical, mental or emotional attributes about yourself would you like to improve to improve your confidence about yourself?

Day 317

What is going well in your life right now? Showing gratitude and appreciation for the things that are working is so important. Take a moment to reflect on the positives.

Day 318

Change is inevitable. Reflect on a minor change that you made in your life that significantly improved your quality life.

Day 319

Clearing your physical space makes room for good energy to flow in. Clutter is heavy and negative energy that weighs your productivity and creativity down. What can you clear out of your physical space today?

Day 320

Do you know your love language? This is important for people in relationships and also single people looking for important qualities in a partner.

Words of affirmation, Acts of Service, Receiving Gifts, Quality Time, Physical Touch.

Learning this can better assist you in learning how to navigate relationships in your life. You can take the test at www.5lovelanguages.com

Day 321

Give yourself a pat on the back.
What is one achievement you are most proud of and why? It can be something big or something small

Day 322

Self improvement is an ongoing process. What are some small wins that you have had so far in your journey?

Day 323

Describe your dream job if money didn't matter. What qualities about this job can you make a reality?

Day 324

Laughter triggers the release of endorphins, the body's natural feel-good chemicals. Endorphins promote an overall sense of well-being.

When is the last time you truly belly laughed?

Day 325

What is something you want to release into the universe? Sometimes just acknowledging these things and jotting them can help better manifest them.

Day 326

Do you practice daily affirmations? Affirmations are positive phrases that can help overcome negative thoughts.

Write out 5 positive affirmations that you can repeat daily.

You have 30 days to go! Really focus in on refining your daily routines and habits. Be sure to reflect how far you have come in this journey as well.

Day 327

"Act the way you'd like to be and soon you'll be the way you act." - George W. Crane

This quote speaks about portraying yourself and acting in ways that align with your core values and end goals, do you believe you do this?

Day 328

Do you have a vision board? Vision boards are a collection of photos and words that represent what you want to manifest into your life. Make it a weekly goal to make a vision board of things you want to bring into your life.

Creating vision boards can be really fun because it gives your mind a visual destination for what you want to bring into your life!

Day 329

What is your favorite way to move your body? Is it swimming? Dancing? Walking? How can you incorporate moving your body everyday? 5 minutes of dancing in the morning? A daily short walk? It is important for both your physical and mental health to exercise or move at least 30 minutes 3-4 days a week.

Day 330

It is proven that having a gratitude journal can decrease stress and improve happiness.

Write down at least one thing you are grateful for in this very moment. This can start a chain reaction for the rest of the day.

Day 331

Take yourself on a mental excursion to the future, what does it look like? Who are you as a person? What have you accomplished? Are you happy?

Day 332

If your thoughts are getting too overwhelming to handle, it may be best to step away and take time out to unwind and get into a calmer state of being. In addition to bringing more awareness to your breath, you can engage in relaxing activities such as meditation, yoga, tai chi, nature walks, listening to soothing music, gardening, drinking calming herbal teas, lighting candles with aromatherapeutic properties, reading a novel, or anything else that brings your pulse down.

When was the last time you stepped away to just be quiet and mindful?

Day 333

Reflection time- at the end of your life what would you want to be remembered as or for. What qualities or accomplishments would be most important to you?

Ask yourself:
What is my life's purpose?
What difference will I make?
How will I be remembered?

Day 334

By constantly preparing and improving yourself, your knowledge, awareness, interpersonal skills you will be that much more prepared to seize great opportunities when they arise.

This quote speaks about always keeping your eyes and mind open for new opportunities to come your way. How do you believe you can be best ready to receive these opportunities?

Day 335

Self-Love

List 10 things that you love about yourself. Come back to this page when you are feeling low and remind yourself of the positive traits you hold.

Day 336

Brain Dump

A brain dump is the act of dumping all the contents of your mind onto paper. Scheduling appointments, things that are nagging you, everything you are feeling. This can release stress and emotions that you are holding onto.

Day 337

What things do people do or don't do that upset you the most? How can you effectively communicate about these things without coming off as angry or upset.

Day 338

Create your MVP list as well (your Most Important Points the week) and start from there. Having an organized to do list for the week significantly helps productivity and making sure no loose ends get away.

Day 339

The first step towards change is awareness. Being aware of where your mind, attention and time is being used.

What actions or behaviors are you aware of in your life that are dragging you down?

Day 340

Adding adventure to your life

When was the last time you did something spontaneous? What adventure would you like to do coming up? It can be something small as a trying a new hiking spot or it can be something bigger like a road trip to go visit an old friend.

Day 341

Mistakes are often life best lessons.
What is a 'mistake' you made that led to an important life lesson or blessing in disguise?

Day 342

Recognizing Jealousy

Have you ever found yourself feeling emotions of jealousy? What was it that you found yourself feeling jealous about? There's no question, that it takes a certain level of emotional maturity to deal with the many feelings around jealousy.

Being able to identify why we are feeling this way can help pinpoint what it is we actually want and why it bothers us.

Day 343

When was a time that you have been in a funk or felt stuck? What tools did you use to help get yourself out of this. There are ups and downs in life and knowing that you can come up from a low always helps.

Staying positive and optimistic can be challenging at times but it is good to know what helps YOU feel better.

Day 344

"Kaizen is everyday improvement every day is a challenge to find a better way of doing things. It needs tremendous self-discipline and commitment."
-Masaaki Imai, Founder of Kaizen Institute

What is one small way you can implement a small Kaizen improvement into your daily routine starting today?

Day 345

Associations and Influences- Who are the people that influence your the most? Your friends, your family?

How do they make you feel?

The people we spend the most time with determine our conversations our attitudes, our opinions.

Day 346

If you want your body to perform at its peak you must be vigilant about only giving it the healthiest and best foods. Do you believe you consume healthy food, what things could you do to have a better and healthier diet?

Make a list of 5 foods you find yourself often cheating on your diet with and a plan of how you can get rid of those foods.

Day 347

Just as you must put healthy and nutritious foods in your body, your mind works the same way. Are you feeding it news, mindless tv shows? Or are you growing and expanding your mind?

Put yourself on a media diet. We often don't realize how many brainless hours we spend scrolling through social media. Set a schedule for yourself of exactly how many minutes you will spent on social media per day and track it in your phone. Make sure you hit your goal or are at least below it.

Day 348

Self-Care Sunday!

How do you spend your Sundays? How can you improve your Sunday routine for a more productive week ahead?

Preparation is key to success, whether it is preparing your mind and body or preparing your meals for the week.

Day 349

Quiet Time

Taking 5 even 10 minutes to reflect on your own thoughts feelings and emotions can have a huge impact on your inner peace. Set aside a time today to be away from your phone, email and tasks to just reflect on you and how you are feeling inside.

Day 350

What is one concrete step you have taken to ensure you stick to your self care or self improvement routine each day? Share what you have learned about yourself and your habit creation patterns.

Day 351

"Good character is developed over time and through the virtues of hard work and commitment. We cannot develop our character without having to work hard and to suffer through times of conflict and challenge. The reason hard work develops character is because it is the only thing that can outdo and outlast both genius and talent." (entrepreneur.com)

What is one obstacle or challenge that you have faced that has truly made your character grow and develop in your life?

Day 352

What keeps you up at night? Is there a pressing problem you need to work out? List 3 steps you can take towards solving this issue today.

Day 353

What is something you respect yourself for? Knowing your self worth and having self respect is an important step in building ones confidence.

Day 354

Do you believe you are in control of your own emotions? What external sources (people, work, situations) often impact your emotional well being? Being aware of your triggers from others gives us power and the control to choose how we respond.

Day 355

What is something you want to release into the universe? What is something you want to call into your life? Sometimes just acknowledging these things can help you to better manifest them.

Day 356

Celebration is important, even in the smallest ways to commemorate an accomplishment, a feat or a new chapter in life. What was the last thing you celebrated? How did it make you feel?

Day 357

Don't chase people. Be a leader and set a good example. Work hard and be your authentic self. The people who belong in your life will come to you. How can you set the best example as a parent, mentor or leader?

Day 358

Where your focus goes, energy flows. Where are you sending your energy? How you send your energy to more things that bring positivity into your life?

Day 359

To be the best partner, parent, mentor you must fulfill your basic needs and give to yourself before giving to others. You cannot pour with an empty cup.
How can you make sure to fill your cup before giving yourself to others?

Day 360

Write a love letter to yourself. Thank yourself for showing up and working towards being the best version of yourself. Be sure to acknowledge the wins and struggles you have faced thus far.

Day 361

Envision yourself 5-10 years down the road you have your dream job, What is your position? What are your responsibilities? How did you reach this goal?

Day 362

What types of exercise, self care and productivity rituals have you enjoyed implementing in your routine the most. How has each of the activities you have tried made you feel? How have you implemented these rituals into your daily/weekly routines?

Day 363

Becoming your ultimate self, not speaking to material possessions, wealth or career in this prompt. Who are you as a person and as a spirit in your ideal end 'ultimate self'. Are you more patient? More nurturing? This can be anything you want to achieve as a being into your self.

Day 364

What is one area in your life you have grown the most over the past year? (health, relationships, finances, career, etc.) What are you more aware or conscious of as a result? Write down the positive ways you have changed and what you have learned or benefited as a result.

On Day 23 I had you jot down 5 words to describe yourself then, after nearly 365 days of improve what 5 words would you use to describe yourself now?

Day 365

Reflection

It has been a long journey, I'm sure filled with many unexpected surprises, some good, some bad. What have you learned the most from this journal? How have you changed or evolved as a person throughout 365 days? What areas did you find the easiest to improve or change? What areas were the hardest for you?

Closing Affirmation

I am headed somewhere incredible in this life. I have so much faith and confidence both in myself and in my abilities. I am grateful for the lessons and challenges I have faced along the way. I have grown and developed as a being. I am stronger, wiser and more aware as a result of my self development. I hold the knowledge and tools I need to create a wonderful life for myself. Each and every day I will focus on becoming the best version of myself.

Share your Transformation story with us @the_kaizen_journal

To learn more about opportunities to work with Kai both in-person or virtually visit kaiboyerfitness.com @KaiBoyer

Kai ♡

Made in the USA
Las Vegas, NV
19 September 2024

95509691R10203